AF211673

D.R. DARRELL

ENHANCE YOUR ENERGY

The Essential Guy On How to Amplify Your Energy, Learn Useful Tips and Steps You Can Take to Increase Your Physical and Mental Energy

Descrierea CIP a Bibliotecii Naționale a României
D.R. DARRELL
    **ENHANCE YOUR ENERGY. The Essential Guy On How
to Amplify Your Energy, Learn Useful Tips and Steps You Can
Take to Increase Your Physical and Mental Energy** / D.R.
Darrell. – Bucharest: Editura My Ebook, 2020
    ISBN 978-606-983-591-3

D.R. DARRELL

ENHANCE YOUR ENERGY

The Essential Guy On How to Amplify Your Energy, Learn Useful Tips and Steps You Can Take to Increase Your Physical and Mental Energy

My Ebook Publishing House
Bucharest, 2020

TABLE OF CONTENTS

INTRODUCTION

Everyone suffers from fatigue and exhaustion in their lives for many different reasons. Whether it's because they work too hard or don't get enough sleep at night, or because they have a lot of mental baggage that drains their energy, or they maintain an unhealthy diet.

For too long we've been living in a society that has trained us to focus outside ourselves for the answers and expend our precious energy creating things externally.

This kind of results-focused mindset causes us to neglect our inner strength and power, which results in us being chronically fatigued and drained of energy.

One thing that everyone needs to get through the daily grind is energy. Without it, we just can't do what we have to do. The most significant difference between people who understand what they want and people who don't is energy. Everything that we do uses up energy.

We expend energy every time we think, perform, or express ourselves. Often, we associate the term energy with the physical variant. However, the fact is that energy is also used for other aspects of daily living.

Both mental and emotional energy is used daily, and in order to keep yourself productive and functional, you have to keep all three aspects energized.

Unfortunately, energy is not something that you can hold onto forever.

With every single action that you take, you expend energy.

Every step that you walk, every moment you think, every ounce of emotion you use, cost you energy, and there will come a time when your energy will become depleted, and you'll become too exhausted to do anything.

If you don't take care of yourself, there will become a time when you can't go on physically, mentally, or emotionally. You'll have exhausted yourself to the limit. This will result in what is known as burnout.

Burnout can have a devastating effect on your performance, including limiting the number of tasks you can complete in a day, the quality of those tasks you are able to complete, and you won't be able to fulfill your commitments.

CHAPTER 1

UNDERSTANDING FATIGUE

Before you can begin to overcome your fatigue, you need first to understand what fatigue is all about. Fatigue is often referred to as lethargy or exhaustion and is that feeling of tiredness and weakness, both physically and mentally.

You can experience temporary fatigue, which is a result of too much work or not getting enough rest. This kind of fatigue can be easily overcome. There is also chronic or medical fatigue, which is more long-term and requires more serious treatment to overcome.

According to research, 10 percent of the world population suffers from fatigue at any given time, with females being affected by fatigue more than males. Most cases of fatigue have underlying mental causes rather than physical causes and one out of five people who suffer fatigue in the United States, states that it affects their normal function and daily lives.

Two Types of Fatigue

There are two kinds of fatigue that you can suffer from, physical fatigue and mental fatigue. Physical fatigue is when you have a hard time doing the things that you usually do, like carrying grocery bags or climbing stairs. Physical exhaustion is just not having enough physical strength to complete daily tasks.

Mental, or psychological fatigue, on the other hand, is when you find it difficult to concentrate on things. In severe cases, you may find even the prospect of getting out of bed to be too much work.

You may feel tired all the time and may also suffer from a lower level of consciousness, which can be extremely dangerous, especially when driving or operating heavy machinery. If you suffer from mental fatigue, you may be mistaken for being drunk or intoxicated.

Weakness

Often times, when referring to fatigue, the words sleepiness and weakness are used to describe the condition.

When the phrase weakness is used, it refers to a situation where your muscles just don't have enough strength to complete even the simplest of physical tasks.

When you experience weakness as a symptom of fatigue, you often need to apply extra effort just to move your arms, legs, and other body parts. This is usually a result of overexerting yourself at some point, like when running a marathon or spending the entire day hiking.

Your body will feel tired and weak, and you'll experience some aches and pains. Fortunately, with enough rest, these symptoms will disappear after a couple of days.

Sleepiness

Sleepiness, also called somnolence, is when you feel sleepy even when you are in the middle of an activity. This can be as a result of not getting enough sleep, which is necessary for you to feel rejuvenated and make you feel more relaxed.

Causes of Fatigue

To overcome fatigue, you must understand the root causes behind it. If you can eliminate the root causes from your life, you can permanently get rid of fatigue from your life. The origins of fatigue can be divided into three main groups; lifestyle, psychological, and medical.

Lifestyle Factors

If you are suffering from fatigue, you may need to look carefully at your lifestyle. Drinking too much alcohol or caffeinated drinks, maintaining unhealthy eating habits, excessive physical work, and activities, and lacking the proper amount of sleep can all contribute to fatigue in your life. To eliminate fatigue from your life, you'll have to consider adjusting your lifestyle.

Psychological Factors

Your fatigue could also be a result of common mental health conditions. If you suffer from depression, stress, anxiety, or are dealing with grief; you can find your energy drained. These common mental health issues can make you feel tired and listless.

Medical Factors

In some instances, a medical condition can leave you feeling exhausted. If you are experiencing chronic fatigue, it is essential to talk to your doctor to determine if you are suffering from a severe medical condition that is resulting in chronic fatigue. Here are some of the common medical conditions that can result in chronic fatigue.

- **Depression** will not only make you feel sad and empty, but it will also drain you of energy. It can cause you to lose sleep, which will result in more fatigue. The first step to correcting this issue is to seek out professional help to address the problem.

- **Diabetes** is the body's inability to produce any or enough insulin to maintain proper sugar levels. While Type 2 diabetes can be controlled with diet and exercise, Type 1 will require medical intervention to keep it under control. Having unstable blood sugar levels can lead to exhaustion and fatigue and can lead to long-term damage to your body.

- **Chronic Fatigue Syndrome** can make you feel certain disabling tiredness that will last for months. Causes can be physical, mental or dietary. However, there is no specific test that can diagnose chronic fatigue syndrome.

- **Sleep Apnea** is a disorder that results in intermittent stopping and starting of your breathing while you sleep. This pattern will cause a lack of oxygen to your body and lack of sleep, leaving you feeling more tired after sleeping than you did before.

- **Toxic Exposure** can leave your feeling drained and fatigued. Chemical solvents, dust, chlorine, and other pollutants and toxins can not only result in chronic fatigue but can also cause long-term damage to your body.

- **Chronic inflammation** is one of the most common causes of fatigue and can be caused by stress, improper diet, injury, and many other things. It is essential to determine the specific cause and get the proper treatment because along with causing fatigue, chronic inflammation can also lead to long-term damage to joints, skin, and other organs.

- **Nutritional Deficiencies** are one of the biggest causes of exhaustion and fatigue. When you are pushed to the limits physically and emotionally, getting the right fuel in your body is extremely important. A proper, balanced diet of fresh fruit and vegetables, lean meat, and grains are imperative for eliminating exhaustion in your life.

To fight fatigue and extreme exhaustion you have to identify the root causes of your condition.

Symptoms of Fatigue

The main sign of fatigue is exhaustion and tiredness, especially after completing a strenuous physical activity or mental exercise. While you may rest after the activity, your mind and body may still feel exhausted. Here are some of the other symptoms of fatigue that you should know if you want to learn how to overcome it.

Physical Symptoms

The physical symptoms of fatigue include sore muscles, dizziness, abdominal pain, headache, bloating, vision problems, and painful lymph nodes. If you experience any of these symptoms for more than two weeks, it is essential to talk to your doctor to rule out any common conditions that can lead to chronic fatigue.

Psychological Symptoms

If you have chronic fatigue, you may suffer from poor concentration, apathy, or a lack of motivation. You may also experience moodiness, indecisiveness, irritability, hallucinations, loss of appetite, memory impairment, poor judgment, slow reflexes and responses to stimuli, sleepiness, or drowsiness.

By knowing these symptoms, you can identify if you are suffering from chronic fatigue or if you are just tired and in need of a good night's sleep. Knowing the symptoms can help you find the right solution so you can get rid of your fatigue and enhance your energy.

CHAPTER 2

CHANGE YOUR DIET AND EATING HABITS

One of the leading causes of chronic fatigue is eating an unhealthy diet. If you eat the wrong kinds of foods often, you can begin to feel tired and overly exhausted. In order to eliminate fatigue and enhance your energy levels, you need to avoid those foods that make you feel tired and heavy.

Consume Food That Give You Energy

When you feel tired, and your energy starts to wane, you may be tempted to reach for the candy bar you have hiding in your desk drawer. While it will give you an instant boost in energy, after about an hour, you'll be right back where you started. Instead of reaching for foods that are high in sugar, you need to eat foods that are high in protein and that contain complex carbohydrates.

Foods that contain complex carbohydrates and are high in protein help to increase your blood glucose levels and keep them at the right level, providing your body with energy for a more extended period. Complex carbohydrates also are digested at a slower rate than simple carbs, resulting in you feeling fuller for longer.

Throughout the day you should try and consume whole grain products like whole wheat bread or whole grain crackers. Add some peanut butter or low-fat cheese and another source of protein to keep you energized throughout the day.

Eat Foods that are Rich in Magnesium

In order to break down the glucose in your blood and turn it into energy, you need to consume Magnesium. Along with converting glucose into energy, magnesium is necessary for the other 300 biochemical processes that take place in your body.

When magnesium levels get too low, your energy level drops significantly, because your glucose isn't being turned into energy properly. Studies have shown that people who have magnesium deficiencies are more likely to tire easily after doing physical tasks.

Having low levels of magnesium can result in easily feeling out of breath and having an increased heart rate. This is an indication that your body is working harder, which can quickly drain your energy and make you feel exhausted.

It is vital that you get the recommended amount of magnesium in your diet if you want to eliminate fatigue. Some excellent sources of magnesium include fish, like halibut, whole grains, almonds, hazelnuts, and cashews.

Eat Small Snacks Between Meals

It is far better for you and your energy level to eat small meals with snacks in between, rather than eating less frequently, but overeating at every meal. This is what is known as power snacking.

By eating small snacks between meals, you keep your blood sugar up and your energy levels high. You can snack on yogurt, fruits, cheese, beef jerky, and nuts to keep you from getting too hungry between meals.

Overeating at meal time isn't good because it can make you feel bloated and heavy, which can result in feeling too lazy to move. To avoid overeating, you may want to consider putting your food on a smaller plate to give the illusion that your plate is full enough and that you are eating a lot.

Drink Plenty of Water

Not only does drinking enough water every day improve your overall health and well-being, but it can help you avoid feeling tired and weak. Water keeps your body hydrated at all times which can help to prevent fatigue. To take full advantage of the power of water, you should consume at least eight cups of water daily. Otherwise, you'll feel sluggish for the entire day.

Include Soluble Fiber in Your Diet

Soluble fiber helps your body absorb sugars more slowly, which is necessary for you to obtain a more sustainable level of energy.

When your body absorbs sugar to quickly, it can lead to a sudden crash soon after the sugar high. You can get soluble fiber from eating nuts, fruits, vegetables, whole grains, oats, and beans.

Use Caffeine in Moderation

Stimulants like coffee, soda, and nicotine can quickly exhaust your adrenaline glands making you feel tired for extended periods of time. Coffee and other caffeinated products can give you the quick energy boost that you need but can become counterproductive if you become dependent on it. If you want to eliminate fatigue, then you have to stop consuming things that give you a quick energy boost.

Eat Foods that Detoxify Your Mind and Body

If you tend to feel tired and exhausted all the time, there are several foods that you can eat to detoxify your body and mind.

Eating cabbage and broccoli will help to cleanse harmful toxins from your liver, and are both rich in antioxidants. Consuming beets can help to cleanse your body while eliminating free radicals. Other foods that can help detoxify your body are:

- Avocados
- Asparagus
- Garlic

- Green Tea

- Lemongrass

- Wheatgrass

Time Your Eating

Properly timing your meals can have a profound effect on your metabolism and energy. Eating too much or too little can make you feel lethargic and can disrupt blood sugar levels, resulting in chronic fatigue. Timing your meals will ensure that you will have enough energy to get through the day and accomplish your tasks without feeling exhausted afterward.

Eat a Satisfying Breakfast and a Lighter Lunch and Dinner

We've all heard the saying, "breakfast is the most important meal of the day," and for a good reason. Breakfast is the first meal of the day and acts as the fuel that you need to keep going. Eating a nutritional breakfast makes you more productive and energetic in the morning and helps to keep you fueled throughout the morning.

If you have a satisfying meal in the morning, you can get away with eating a lighter lunch and dinner. Overeating in the afternoons and evening can make you feel sluggish and actually diminish the energy you have to get you through the rest of the day.

Maintaining a well-balanced diet and consuming the right kinds of foods at the right times throughout the day can help you eliminate fatigue and enhance your energy levels. Following the above advice will keep your energy levels high throughout the day and allow you to accomplish more in your day.

CHAPTER 3

CHANGE YOUR LIFESTYLE

Another cause of fatigue can be contributed to having a poor lifestyle. The wrong kind of lifestyle will cause fatigue and exhaustion, as well as leading to a number of other health problems in your life.

You may not know it but the things that you do every day could be contributing to your constant fatigue and exhaustion. To work toward finally getting rid of fatigue, you need to know how to change your lifestyle to keep your energy levels high.

Get Enough Exercise

One of the fundamentals of energy management is learning how to take care of your body. Taking care of it well, allows you to keep the pace for more extended periods. One of the essential aspects of taking care of your body is exercising.

You may think that trying to exercise when you are tired is counterproductive. However, exercising is extremely useful in fighting fatigue. Exercise helps to improve your endurance and muscle strength, which makes you feel less tired as time goes by.

It also helps to distribute the nutrients and oxygen to your cells, which allow your body to work more efficiently. When your body works more efficiently, you don't feel as tired when you participate in physical activity because your body doesn't have to work double time.

Benefits of Exercising

- It keeps your body in excellent condition, which is one of the biggest keys to keeping your energy levels up. When you get enough physical exercise, you develop physical endurance. This is especially true when you participate in a cardio workout. By merely getting into shape, you can have more energy to survive the daily grind.

- It's an outlet for stress release. Stress can not only make you fed up physically, but it can cause you to become fed up both mentally and emotionally. Having an outlet to release tension is extremely important for keeping your stable. There are many ways you can release stress, but one of the best ways is to engage in physical exercise.

- It can help you sculpt your body. As your muscles become more defined, your body works more efficiently.

- It can relieve you of the effects of chronic fatigue. Fatigue can have a devastating impact on your life. One of the best ways to reduce the impact of fatigue is to exercise regularly. Regular exercise strengthens your muscles and joints that may be worn out with repetitive work.

There are many ways that you can increase your levels of physical activity to help enhance your energy. You can head to the gym, you can head out for a jog in the morning or evenings, or you can participate in a sport on the weekends. Here are some other forms of exercise that you can do to help you overcome exhaustion.

Yoga

Practicing yoga will not only help increase your energy, but it is also excellent for regaining your balance. Practicing yoga on a regular basis can help you deal with stress and decrease the symptoms of depression. It is known to help improve flexibility, as well as increase metabolic rate while boosting your cardiovascular health.

Running or Walking

Walking and running are great ways to get your heart pumping and your body moving. Along with increasing your energy levels, running or walking can help to improve your overall health and aids in the prevention of many diseases.

Creating a running or walking habit can help to relieve stress, which can quickly kill your energy levels. These forms of exercise can also reduce symptoms of depression. Along with giving you an instant boost in energy, it can also help to clear your mind.

Tai Chi

Tai Chi is one of the most popular kinds of exercises in the East. Tai Chi can increase your vitality and help you combat stress. It can also improve your cognitive function while effectively elevating your energy levels.

It is also known to improve your quality of sleep, which is enormous when it comes to restoring your energy and vitality.

Dancing

Dancing is one of the most enjoyable forms of exercise. It can help you to combat stress while toning your muscles. Dancing is also one of the most effective ways to manage your weight.

Participating in an organized dance lesson or just going out for a fun night of dancing on a Friday night can make you feel happy, which can be extremely beneficial when you are fighting fatigue.

You don't have to commit to intense workouts to benefit from the physical activity. Something as simple as changing your usual sedentary routine can do a lot for your energy and overall health. Consider taking the stairs rather than hopping on the elevator, or park farther away from the store entrance when out shopping.

You can also try new hobbies that involve physical activity, like playing sports, hiking, or biking. These simple and fun activities can help make your body stronger and decrease fatigue. As you begin to become more physically active, you will notice a substantial increase in your energy, making completing your daily tasks much easier.

Get Enough Rest and Sleep

Another reason you may be suffering from fatigue and exhaustion is that you aren't getting enough rest and restorative sleep. If you try to do too many tasks at one time, you'll end up feeling physically and mentally tired, which can quickly lead to fatigue. This is why it is so important to give your body and mind a break and time to recover after doing something that is particularly stressful or tiring.

On average, most people require eight hours of sleep every night to avoid fatigue. To ensure you get the sleep you need, it is essential to set a regular bedtime and wake up at the same time every day to allow your body to get used to the routine.

When you get enough sleep at night, you will naturally wake up, without having to rely on setting the alarm. It is much better for your physical and mental health to wake up on your own, rather than relying on an alarm.

If for some reason, you aren't able to get eight hours of sleep, you can make up for the lost sleep hours by taking a nap during the day. This will allow you to catch up on sleep without disrupting your regular sleep patterns.

Another way to keep yourself from becoming overly fatigued is to rest your body and mind after completing tasks. Utilize breaks at work wisely to become more efficient and productive. When you are doing household chores, be sure to take a break so you can reenergize your body.

Get Rid of Vices and Bad Habits

Your bad habits, like drinking alcohol, smoking, or consuming too much sugar and caffeine, can significantly contribute to your fatigue. Alcohol has a sedative effect that results in your body feeling heavy. You should avoid having an afternoon drink, especially if you still have a lot of tasks to complete before calling it a day.

You may be in the habit of drinking alcohol after dinner or before you go to bed because you think that it helps you sleep better.

However, alcohol prevents your mind and body from going into a deep sleep, resulting in you not feeling rested and refreshed, even if you get the recommended eight hours of sleep at night.

Smoking can also zap your energy because it prevents you from getting a good night's sleep. People who quit smoking have claimed that their energy levels double, and sometimes triple, after getting rid of the bad habit. Smoking can cause you to feel moody, cranky, and irritable throughout the day, which can drain your energy. If you want to enhance your energy and eliminate fatigue, you need to find a way to quit smoking.

Along with affecting your energy and causing you to be more fatigues, alcohol consumption and smoking can have other adverse effects on your body that can significantly impact your health.

Engage in a Relaxing Hobby

Along with participating in hobbies that require you to expend energy, like hiking, dancing, or a variety of sports, you should also engage in hobbies that are relaxing. Hobbies that promote relaxation are great for when you need to unwind after a long day at work or an afternoon of strenuous activity.

Rather than reaching for the TV remote or video game controller when you need to relax, you need to find a relaxing activity like gardening or reading. Unfortunately, TV and video games require your mind to continue to work, which can increase your stress, even if you are just sitting on the couch.

Engaging in relaxing activities like baking or woodworking will relax both your mind and body because they don't require you to overthink and are not physically strenuous.

Practice Meditation

Meditation is a powerful tool that you can use to help you manage your stress and eliminate fatigue, and improve the overall quality of your life. It has also been shown to improve your cognitive function and increase your energy and vitality when practiced regularly.

When you practice meditation regularly, you are in fact, training your body to relax. When you rest, you lower the levels of cortisol that your body is producing. Cortisol is known as the stress hormone because it is released when you become stressed. High levels of cortisol in your blood are associated with fatigue, increased blood pressure, stress, and weight gain.

If you are just starting out with meditation, here's how to get the most benefit from each session.

- Sit or lie comfortably. You may want to invest in a good meditation chair or cushion to ensure that you are comfortable throughout the entire session.

- Close your eyes.

- Breathe naturally. Try to avoid trying to control your breathing. Just inhale and exhale as you usually would.

- Start to focus your attention on your breath and how your body moves with every inhalation and exhalation. Notice the movement of your body as you breathe. Observe your chest, shoulders, rib cage, and belly. Focus your attention on your breathing, avoiding trying to control its pace or intensity. If you find that your mind is wandering, return your focus back to your breath.

Maintain your meditation for two to three minutes when you are first starting out. Once you find that you can maintain your focus for at least three minutes, you can start to increase the time of each session. There are no real downsides to meditation and can be incredibly relaxing and help relieve symptoms of fatigue.

Listen to Relaxing Music

Recent studies have shown that listening to soothing music can reduce stress, anxiety, and fatigue. It has also been shown to help you get a good night's sleep, effectively reducing the effects of insomnia, which can help you further fight fatigue.

Music helps to calm us down, relax our muscles, reduce stress, decrease blood pressure, and improve the heart rate. It works similarly as meditation. To help eliminate stress and increase your energy, try listening to soothing music, like Bach, in the mornings and before you go to bed at night.

CHAPTER 4

ORGANIZE YOUR LIFE

One thing that can cause you to become fatigued is chaos and clutter in your life. If you want to be free of fatigue and exhaustion, then you need to keep your home, workspace, and life, in general, organized. There are a variety of things that you can do to create a more organized life.

Create Lists

Writing down everything that you need to accomplish and remember throughout the day makes it easier for you to perform your daily tasks. Trying to remember everything that you need to achieve during the day can drain your energy. By creating lists, you eliminate the need to make an effort memorizing and remembering everything you have to do.

When you go grocery shopping, you need to make a list of the things that you need to buy so that you don't have to expend energy trying to remember what you need. At the end of the day, create a list of the tasks that you need to accomplish the following day.

Another list you should consider making is one of your monthly expenses so that you can plan your budget. You can write your lists in a small notebook or organizer, or utilize one of the many organization apps for your smartphone. Whichever you choose, just make sure you're creating your lists every day.

Create Schedules and Deadlines

Another way you can better organize your life is by creating schedules and deadlines for all the things that you need to do. This can help you avoid wasting your time, which will give you the time you need to rest and relax and replenish your energy. If you aren't able to manage your time effectively, you'll only end up trying to finish everything at the last minutes which can make you feel exhausted.

By creating schedules and deadlines for yourself, you know what needs to be done, and you can focus your attention on one task at a time. It's important to remember to set reasonable deadlines and schedules to avoid becoming more stressed and tired.

Avoid Procrastinating

Falling into a habit of procrastination only makes your tasks more difficult when it's time to complete them. Procrastinating just makes you more stressed because you have to rush things to meet the deadlines that you set for yourself. Procrastination will also cause you to produce low-quality results.

If you begin your tasks at the earliest possible time, you can take more time to complete them without having to finish them in a short amount of time. Also, when you can finish a task before its deadline, it gives you even more time to sit back and relax and replenish your energy.

When you create a schedule and set deadlines, it is crucial that you stick with it. To help eliminate fatigue you need to learn how to focus on completing the task at hand and avoid distractions, like checking your email, social media, or answering the phone.

Prioritize

While creating a schedule is a good thing, along to-do-list can become overwhelming. To avoid becoming fatigued at the thought of completing everything on your schedule, you need to learn how to prioritize. To help you prioritize the tasks that you need to complete, take a look at your list and decide which jobs have to be completed that day and which ones can be moved to another day.

For example, if its June and you included shopping for school supplies on your list of things to do, along with everything else that you need to finish, you may begin to feel overwhelmed and too exhausted by the time you reach the end of your list.

To fix this, move the task of shopping for school supplies, and other functions that you don't need to complete right away, to another day, giving you the time to complete the tasks with the nearest deadline.

De-Clutter Your Workspace

Another way to keep your life organized is to de-clutter your workspace. Getting rid of clutter at your desk will help you become more efficient throughout the day. Before you leave for the day, make it a point to clear off the surface of your desk, making sure to put everything back where it belongs. Don't leave files and folders piled on top of your desk.

Instead, designate a tray for all your incoming and outgoing documents. Place any materials that you don't need immediately into a file cabinet. It will be much easier for you to work when everything is put in its proper place, so you don't have to waste time searching for items you need.

De-Clutter Your Home

If you want to have a place to rest and relax, then you'll have to de-clutter your home. A clean and well-organized house will make it much easier for you to relax your tired mind and body. Having a cluttered home will only lead to you feeling more stressed out and tired, which can be a contributing factor to your fatigue and exhaustion. You have to get rid of your home's clutter if you want to work toward eliminating fatigue from your life.

While it will take some time and effort up front, de-cluttering your home now will be well worth it when you can finally eliminate fatigue from your life. Start by going through your things and getting rid of anything that you no longer need or have any use for, like old clothes, toys, DVDs, or books.

You can either donate the items to charity or hold a yard sale. If you find things that are broken and that are beyond repair, throw them out. At the end of the day, you only want to have items in your home that you still use.

To keep your house clutter-free, you need to have a place to put everything. You should utilize shelves, drawers, and cabinets to minimize the clutter and make it easier to find what you are looking for. You also want to limit the number of things that you purchase. Before you buy anything, you need to ask yourself if it is something that you really need.

Learn to Delegate

Another great way to stop yourself from becoming fatigued is to delegate tasks. Understanding that you don't have to do everything yourself can be extremely beneficial in reducing exhaustion and enhancing your energy. You can delegate tasks both at work and in your personal life. If you are a manager of a supervisor, learn how to delegate tasks to your employees appropriately. When you are at home, enlist the help of your kids and other household members to complete chores. It is vital that you make sure that you also take care of your responsibilities and not depend on others to do everything for you.

Learn the Power of 'No'

To prevent fatigue, you need to learn what your limitations are both physically and mentally. It is important that you learn how to say 'no' if you don't think that you can take on any more tasks or responsibilities.

You don't have to work overtime whenever your boss asks you to, and you don't have to participate in every social engagement that comes up. You need to learn how to pay attention to your body and learn how to decline invitations and requests politely.

CHAPTER 5

AVOID STRESS

If you want to avoid fatigue, then you need to learn about the different stress management techniques that can help you manage your emotions. When stress is left unmanaged, it can quickly drain you of all your energy.

Extreme levels of stress can be hazardous if you don't take the time to deal with the issue immediately. It can affect your cognitive function and energy levels, as well as changing the overall quality of your life. It is imperative if you want to eliminate fatigue and enhance your energy to learn how to minimize stress in your life.

Don't be Too Hard on Yourself

Most of the stress that we experience in our lives is self-induced. If you want to combat stress and eliminate fatigue from your life, then you have to avoid being too hard on yourself.

Avoid burning the candle at both ends. Take the time to relax and recharge yourself and avoid working too hard and pushing yourself to the point of extreme exhaustion.

Get Rid of the Notion of Perfectionism

Many people continuously aim for perfectionism. The problem with this is that you are continually setting yourself up to fail by setting unrealistic standards for yourself. One of the most powerful ways you can deal with stress and anxiety in your life is to drop the notion of perfectionism.

However, you always want to remember to try your hardest and do the best you can each time you focus on a task. The important part is recognizing that your best is good enough.

Don't Take Yourself Too Seriously

This life is complicated enough as it is, don't add to your stress by taking life and yourself too seriously. If you aim to live a happy and stress-free life, you have to develop a great sense of humor.

It is vital that you learn to laugh at yourself. There is always something funny in every situation that you find yourself in, even the most difficult circumstances. Finding the humor in life will help you feel better and will instantly increase your energy.

Talk to Someone

Enlist the help of a professional. Talking to someone about your life, both the good and bad aspects of it, can help you manage your stress and increase the amount of energy you have every day.

Speaking with a professional can help you realize that you aren't alone in your fears and problems. Talking to someone that you trust can be incredibly therapeutic and help you learn how to manage your stress better.

Be Clear About Your Goals

To avoid spreading yourself too thin and avoid excess stress, it is essential that you are clear about what you want to achieve. Start setting clear goals in every area of your life, including personal development, career, finances, health, and relationships. Knowing exactly what you need to do to achieve your goals will keep you from becoming overly stressed and exhausted.

Stop Trying to Control Everything

There are going to be things that come up in your life that you can't control. If you want to live a happy, stress-free, and high energy life, then you need to focus your energy on those things in your life that you can control and learn to let go of the things that you can't control.

Take Deep Breaths

When you are feeling stressed or overly fatigued, taking a few slow, deep breaths will help you to relax. Take a moment to breathe in as far as you can, and exhale as much as you can. Do this 3-5 times, slowly, and you will feel the effects on your stress levels and fatigue immediately.

Aside from managing your stress, you need to learn how to control your emotions if you want to eliminate fatigue and enhance your energy. Negative emotions, like anger, jealousy, resentment, and guilt will drain your energy and increase your levels of anxiety, fatigue, and result in depression.

Negative emotions can expend all your energy, and it can suck out all the positivity in your life. Learning how to control your emotions will reduce your fatigue and increase your energy.

Forgive Yourself

If you always feel guilty about things that you've done in the past, you will only increase your levels of exhaustion and stress. You have to learn to forgive yourself for your past mistakes and misgivings if you want to live a life free of stress and fatigue.

When you learn to forgive yourself, you will see an immediate increase in your vitality and energy, as well as improved health.

Forgive Others

One of the quickest ways to drain your energy and create anxiety in your life is to hold onto grudges. For you to increase your energy and vitality, you have to learn to forgive those who have hurt you in the past.

Forgiving them doesn't mean that you are condoning their actions and it doesn't mean that you have to welcome them back into your life. Forgiveness simply means that you are ready to let go of the past hurt and that you are prepared to live the life that you deserve.

Create Healthy Personal Boundaries

You may feel like you want to please everyone around you. However, trying to please everyone, all the time can become incredibly frustrating and lead to increased levels of stress and fatigue. If you want to improve your emotions and increase your energy, you need to create healthy personal boundaries.

Engaging in people-pleasing behavior often drains your energy because you end up spreading yourself too thin. Remember, it's okay to say no to requests that don't serve your best interests.

Creating healthy personal boundaries is one of the most powerful ways that you can prevent stress in your life and eliminate fatigue.

You have to learn how to manage your stress and emotions if you want to live a high energy life. If you find it impossible to avoid some stressful situations, then it is in your best interest to deal with these situations as lightly and as objectively as you can.

CONCLUSION

When facing chronic fatigue, the first thing that you should do is rule out any medical condition that you may have. If you do have one of the many medical conditions that contribute to chronic fatigue, the best thing you can do is take your doctor's advice and follow any treatment plan they recommend.

If a medical condition has been ruled out as a reason for your constant fatigue, then it's likely that your current lifestyle is contributing to your exhaustion. The good news is that it can be reversed and you can increase your energy, both physically and mentally.

Focusing on changing your lifestyle and doing what you can to eliminate stress from your life will help you to enhance your energy and rebuild your vitality, removing fatigue from your life for good.

While you probably won't be able to markedly change your entire lifestyle overnight, you can easily concentrate on a few of the more important things first. Even the smallest changes in your lifestyle will help to improve your energy, allowing you to continue to make positive changes to your lifestyle that will affect your everyday life.

To effectively combat fatigue and enhance your energy, you just need to take things one day at a time and focus on becoming a better version of yourself. Each small change that you make will have a significant impact on your overall health, energy, and vitality. You don't have to continue to live with exhaustion and fatigue.

Making simple changes in your daily life and diet, can help you find the energy you need to make it through your days. There is nothing like being able to live a full and productive live with enough energy to get through even the most challenging of tasks.

Printed by Libri Plureos GmbH in Hamburg, Germany